Microsoft® Office 365
Office 2016

D0088319

Welcome to Microsoft® Office 365 & Office 2016

Microsoft Office 2016 is the newest version of the Office productivity suite. It can be purchased as a one-time purchase or through a subscription plan known as Office 365. With an Office 365 subscription plan you get the Office programs—Word, Excel, PowerPoint, OneNote, Outlook, Publisher (PC only), and Access (PC only)—which can be installed across multiple devices, including iPads, and iPhones.

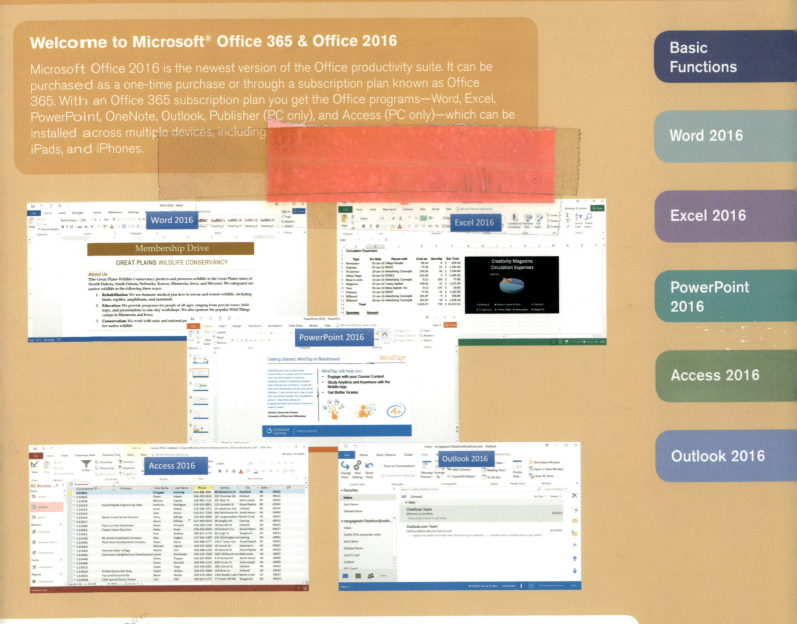

Basic Functions

Word 2016

Excel 2016

PowerPoint 2016

Access 2016

Outlook 2016

What's New in Microsoft Office 365 & Office 2016?

- Simplified sharing right from your Office application in Word, Excel, and PowerPoint.
- Work with others simultaneously using the new co-authoring feature in Word and PowerPoint.
- Six new chart types in Word, Excel, and PowerPoint that help you visualize common financial, statistical, and hierarchical data.
- Type what you want to do in the Tell Me box and the app will assist you in finding the commands you are looking for.
- Highlight a word and Smart Lookup will search the web for definitions, images, and other online resources using Bing.
- Enhanced OneDrive integration gives you access to your Office documents from anywhere or any device.

Office 2016 opens with a color-coded Start screen unique to each application with the exception of Outlook. It displays your recent documents, blank document selection, template options, or the Open Other Documents option, which searches for a document in a local or OneDrive folder. The Start screen assists you in finding all your documents in one place. The upper-right corner of the Start screen displays the current OneDrive Account.

Open an existing file

1. On the Start screen, click Open Other Documents.
2. In the Open dialog box, browse to select the appropriate folder. Select the file you want to open, and then click Open.

Save a file to your local drive

1. Click the File tab to open Backstage View.
2. Click Save As and select This PC.
3. Click Browse and navigate to the location you wish to save the file.
4. Type a name for the file, and then click Save.

Save and share your file via OneDrive

1. Click the Share button ⏣ Share in the top-right corner of the ribbon.
2. Select Save to Cloud and choose a location on your OneDrive account to save your file.
3. In the text field under Invite people, enter the email address of the person you would like to share with.

Print a file

1. Click the File tab to open Backstage View and then click Print.
2. Set printing options such as the number of copies to print, printer selection, orientation, and paper size.
3. Click Print.

Note: A print preview image will be displayed on the right side. To view each page of the document, click the arrows below the image.

Close a file

1. Click the File tab to open the Backstage View.
2. Click Close.

Note: If you have made changes to the current file and have not yet saved them, you will be prompted to do so at this point.

Use the Tell Me box for assistance

The Tell Me box is a new feature that allows you to enter words and phrases about what you want to do next and quickly get to features you want to use or actions you want to perform.

> 💡 Tell me what you want to do...

1. Type your question into the Tell Me box located above the ribbon.
2. Choose one of the suggestions or choose Get Help to open the Help dialog box.

Get help

1. Click the File tab to open Backstage View.
2. Click the ? in the upper right corner.
3. In the Help dialog box, type your question or search term in the search box, and then press Enter.

Note: You can also bring up the Help dialog box by pressing F1 on your keyboard.

Define a word or phrase using Smart Lookup

Smart Lookup automatically finds information on the web using Bing's search engine without opening a browser.

1. Select a word or phrase in your document and right-click.
2. Click Smart Lookup in the pop-up menu.
3. The Insights pane will appear on the right with definitions, Wiki articles, and top related searches from the web.

Check your spelling

1. Click the Review tab.
2. In the Proofing group, click Spelling & Grammar.
3. Use the displayed message to correct any errors.

Note: In Access, click the Home tab.

Find and replace text

1. Click Replace in the upper-right corner of the ribbon.
2. In the Find what box, type the word or phrase to find all instances of that word or phrase.
3. In the Replace with box, type the replacement text.
4. Click Replace All or Replace.

Use the Format Painter in Word

Use the Format Painter to quickly copy formatting from one item to another. This works similar in other programs, such PowerPoint and Excel.

1. Select the text or graphic that has the formatting that you want to copy.
2. On the Home tab, in the Clipboard group, click Format Painter. The pointer changes to a paintbrush 🖌.
3. Select the text or graphic you want to apply the formatting to.

Note: If you would like to apply formatting to more than one area, double click the Format Painter icon. To turn this off again, click the Format Painter again.

File Name Conventions

The Microsoft Office default extensions for each application are as follows:

- Word—.docx
- Excel—.xlsx
- PowerPoint—.pptx
- Access—.accdb

Cut, Copy, and Paste

In each of the Office applications you can move text or objects around using the cut, copy, and paste commands. Cutting or copying selected text or objects places it in a temporary storage area called the Clipboard until you are ready to paste it into your document.

Cut and paste text

When you cut and paste you are moving the text from one location to another.

1. Highlight the text you want to cut.
2. On the Home tab, in the Clipboard group, click Cut to cut the selected information to the Office Clipboard.
   Note: You can also press CTRL+X or right-click on the selected information and then click Cut to copy to the Clipboard.
3. Click where you want to paste the text.
4. On the Home tab, in the Clipboard group, click the Paste button.

Excel 2016

Excel 2016 is a spreadsheet application you use to track, analyze, and perform calculations on numerical data. Excel can recommend which chart is best for showcasing your data. Excel includes a number of functions that make quick work of very complex what-if calculations, such as determining a monthly loan payment amount for different loan amounts and interest rates.

Create a workbook
1. Open Excel 2016 to view the Start screen.
2. If you want to start from a blank workbook, click Blank workbook in the templates pane.
3. If you want to start with a template, type a search term in the Search for online templates text box or use one of the templates available in the templates pane, and then click Create.

Insert a formula
A formula is an expression which calculates the value of a cell. Excel uses standard mathematical operators for formulas, such as a plus sign (+) for addition, a minus sign (-) for subtraction, an asterisk (*) for multiplication, a forward slash (/) for division, and a caret (^) for exponents. All formulas in Excel must begin with an equal sign (=).

	A
1	12
2	23
3	=A1+A2

1. Select the cell that will contain the formula.
2. Type the equal sign (=).
3. Type the formula into the cell —For example A1+A2
4. Press Enter.

Sum data using AutoSum
If you have a complete column or row of numbers to add, use AutoSum. When you click AutoSum, Excel automatically enters a formula—that uses the SUM function—to sum the numbers.

A
Quantity
35
78
56
90
=SUM(A2:A5)

1. Click the cell at the end of the list you want to add.
2. On the Home tab, in the Editing group, click AutoSum Σ ·.
3. Ensure that the correct range of numbers is selected and then press Enter.

Select a format for a cell or range of cells
1. Select the cells or range of cells for which you want to apply a format.
2. On the Home tab, in the Number group, click the Number Dialog Box Launcher to open the Format Cells dialog box.
3. Select the format you want to use.

Insert a chart
1. Highlight the range(s) of cells containing your data, including the headings, to display the Quick Analysis button to the lower right of your data.
2. Click the Quick Analysis button to display the Quick Analysis gallery.
3. Click Charts to view the recommended charts to help you visualize your data.
4. Click one of the recommended chart options or click More Charts, to find your desired chart type.

	House 1	House 2	House 3	House 4	House 5
Asking Price	$150,000	$229,000	$275,000	$325,000	$335,000
Bedrooms	4	4	4	3	4
Bathrooms	2.5	2.25	3		
Year built	1913	1981	20		
Size (in sq. ft.)	2,950	2,600	3,0		

Formatting | Charts | Totals | Tables | Sparklines

Clustered Column | Line | Pie | Clustered Bar | Stacked Area | More Charts

Recommended Charts help you visualize data.

PowerPoint 2016

PowerPoint 2016 is a presentation application you use to create slide shows, which can include charts, tables, pictures, SmartArt, and animation. You can also display your slide shows on a local computer, create a video from the slides, or even broadcast your presentation over the Internet to share with others.

Create a new presentation from a design template
1. Open PowerPoint 2016 to view the Start screen.
2. Type a search term in the Search for online templates text box or use one of the templates available in the templates pane, and then click Create.

Insert a slide into a presentation
1. On the Home tab, in the Slides group, click New Slide.
2. In the gallery, click the layout you want to use for the new slide.

Change the layout of a slide
1. In the Slides pane, select the slide for which you want to change the layout.
2. On the Home tab, in the Slides group, click Layout.
3. In the displayed gallery, click the layout you want to use for the new slide.

Insert an object into a slide
1. Click the appropriate slide to select it.
2. On the Insert tab, in the Illustrations group, click the Shapes, SmartArt, or Chart button to add one of these objects.
3. As prompted, define the relevant options for the type of object selected.

Show your presentation in Presenter View

Use Presenter View to view your notes while delivering your presentation. To show your presentation in Presenter View:
1. Open the presentation that you want to view.
2. On the Slide Show tab, in the Start Slide Show group, click the From Beginning button. Your slide show begins from the first slide, in Full Screen mode.
3. In the Slide Show view, in the lower-left corner of the screen, click the three dots (…), and then click Show Presenter View.

Office Mix

About Office Mix
Office Mix is a free PowerPoint add-in from Microsoft that adds features to PowerPoint. Using Office Mix, you can record presentations, draw on slides, insert quizzes, polls, videos, screen captures, and screen recordings which PowerPoint "mixes" into what Microsoft describes as "an interactive, playable presentation" that you can then view on the Office Mix website. Once your presentation is complete, you can upload to the Office Mix website to publish and share the link. Mixes can be watched on any device with an Internet connection and a web browser.

Download and install Office Mix
1. Log on to the Office Mix website at https://mix.office.com.
2. Click Sign In at the top right portion of the screen.
3. Sign in with an organizational account if your organizaton uses Office 365, or sign in with your Microsoft, Google, or Facebook account.
4. Once logged in, click Get Office Mix.
5. Once Office Mix is installed, a new tab is added to the PowerPoint ribbon called Mix.

Word 2016

Word 2016 is both a word processor and a desktop publishing program for creating documents. You can easily add references to insert citations into your document as well as use styles to create a table of contents. New features include the ability to create, open, edit, and save documents to the cloud.

Create a document

1. Open Word 2016 to view the Start screen.
2. If you want to start with a blank document, click the Blank document thumbnail in the templates pane.
3. If you want to start with a template, type a search term in the Search for online templates text box, or use one of the templates available in the templates pane and click Create.

Define page settings

1. Click the Layout tab.
2. To set the page orientation, in the Page Setup group, click Orientation. Click Portrait or Landscape.
3. To set the page margins, in the Page Setup group, click Margins. Click one of the predefined margin settings or click Custom Margins to set the margins manually.
4. To select a paper size, in the Page Setup group, click Size. Click a paper size. If you want to define a custom paper size, click More Paper Sizes.

Add a page number to a document footer

1. Double-click in the footer of the document. The Header and Footer contextual tab will appear with the Design tab selected.
2. In the Header and Footer group, click Page Number, and then Current Position. Select the desired page numbering style to add the page numbering.

Format a picture using layout options

1. Click a picture in your Word document.
2. Click the Layout Options icon to the upper-right of the picture to view the Layout Options box.
3. To wrap text around the picture, click one of the With Text Wrapping options. Or to keep the picture in line with the text, click the In Line with Text option.
4. Click the Move with text option if you want to ensure the picture moves as the text shifts.

Add a new source and insert a citation

1. To add a citation, verify that the insertion point is where you want to insert the citation.
2. On the References tab, in the Citations & Bibliography group, click the down arrow on the Insert Citation button.
3. Click Add New Source.
4. In the Create Source dialog box, select the type of citation (such as Web site) from the Type of Source list, and then fill in the relevant fields.
5. Click OK.

Note: Word stores your citations in a master citation list. This means that after you have added a source, you can use it again in any of your documents simply by selecting it from the master list.

Edit a source

1. On the References tab, in the Citations & Bibliography group, click Manage Sources.
2. Select the appropriate citation, and then click Edit.
3. Make the necessary changes to the citation.
4. Click OK to save your changes.

Use a citation from your master list in a new document

1. On the References tab, in the Citations & Bibliography group, click Manage Sources.
2. Under Master List, select the appropriate citation and then click Copy to add the citation to your current document.
3. Verify that your insertion point is where you want to insert the citation.
4. In the Citations & Bibliography group, click the arrow on the Insert Citation button. Click the appropriate citation to insert it in your document.

Create a bibliography or works cited list

1. Place the insertion point on the page you want to create the bibliography—usually on a blank page at the end of the document.
2. On the References tab, in the Citations & Bibliography group, click Bibliography. Click the type of bibliography you want to create. Word automatically inserts the bibliography wherever you placed your insertion point.

Use styles to create a table of contents

You can create a table of contents by applying heading styles to the text to include in the table of contents. Word searches for those headings and then inserts the table of contents into your document. When you create the table of contents this way you can automatically update the table of contents if you make changes to your document.

1. Apply heading styles—Heading 1 and Heading 2, for example— to the text that you want to include in the table of contents.
2. Click in the document you want to insert the table of contents— usually on a blank page near the beginning of a document.
3. On the References tab, in the Table of Contents group, click Table of Contents. Select an Automatic table from the list.
4. A table of contents will be generated in your document based on the headings in your document.

Note: If you change any of the headings, or insert new ones you can update the table. All you need to do is to click on the table and choose the Update Table... option.

ISBN-13: 978-1-305-96999-5
ISBN-10: 1-305-96999-5
9 781305 969995   90000

W6-BZY-079

Copy and paste text

When you copy and paste you are not moving the text from one location but making a duplicate of the text to be copied to another location.

1. Highlight the text you want to copy.
2. On the Home tab, in the Clipboard group, click Copy to copy the selected information to the Office Clipboard.

Note: You can also press CTRL+C or right-click on the selected information and then click Copy to copy to the Clipboard.

3. Click where you want to paste the text.
4. On the Home tab, in the Clipboard group, click the Paste button.

Online Pictures

About online pictures

In Microsoft Office 2016, online pictures can be inserted directly into your Word documents, Excel spreadsheets, PowerPoint presentations, and Outlook email messages. When you click the Insert tab and then Online Pictures, by default you are taken to Bing which searches Creative Commons for your image. Creative Commons licensing allows you to use the image provided that you follow the licensing guidelines for the image. Always click the web link for the image and verify the licensing. Check for any copyrights or other restrictions before using an image. If you are unsure of whether an image has restrictions on its use, it is best to not use the image.

Insert online pictures from Bing

1. On the Insert tab, in the Illustrations group, click Online Pictures.
2. Enter a search term in the Bing search box, and then press Enter.
3. Verify the license by clicking on the web link. Look for a statement that the image is free to use without restrictions.
4. If it is free to use, click on the image and then click Insert.

Themes

Themes format a document to have consistent fonts, font characteristics, (such as typeface, size, and color), lines and fill effects. The advantage of using themes is they enable you to quickly and consistently format a document, spreadsheet, or presentation.

Apply a theme

1. In Word, click the Design tab. In the Document Formatting group, click Themes to display the theme gallery. In Excel, on the Page Layout tab, in the Themes group, click Themes. In PowerPoint, on the Design tab, in the Themes group, click the More button.
2. Preview the changes a theme makes to your document by pointing to each theme.
3. When you have determined which theme you want to use, click the theme to apply it.

Define custom theme colors

1. On the Design tab in Word or the Page Layout tab in Excel, click Colors. In PowerPoint, on the Design tab, in the Variants group, click the More button, and then click Colors.
2. Click Customize Colors.
3. Use the lists associated with each element to select the colors you want to use.

4. When you are finished, in the Custom text box, type a name for your color scheme.
5. Click OK to save your changes. The Office application immediately applies your new color scheme to your document.

Styles

About styles

Styles contain predefined settings for text (including colors, fonts, and effects) within a document. You use these style components such as titles, headings, subheadings, and body text. Each theme you select comes with its own set of styles for text, but where you apply these styles is up to you. Styles are only available in Word and Excel. The styles available vary in both applications.

Apply a style

1. Select the text to which you want to apply a style. (In Excel, select one or more cells.)
2. On the Home tab (Word), in the Styles group, click the More drop-down arrow. Click the desired style. On the Home tab (Excel), in the Styles group, click the Cell Styles drop-down arrow. Click the desired style.

Screen Clipping

Word, Excel, PowerPoint, and Outlook allow you to capture a screen clipping of a website or screen shot into your document without leaving the program.

Add a screen clipping to a document

1. In Word, Excel, and Outlook, click the Insert tab. In the Illustrations group, click Screenshot. In PowerPoint, on the Insert tab, in the Images group, click Screenshot.
2. To add a portion of the screen, click Screen Clipping.
3. With the cross-shaped cursor, select the area you want to appear in your document.

Office Add-ins

About Office Add-ins

You can use add-ins to extend the functionality of a document, spreadsheet, email message, or database. Each application has different add-ins available at the Microsoft Store. There are add-ins to help you learn about the various Office program features, look up words in a dictionary, and even to create live interactive maps in your Excel spreadsheets. Many of the Office Add-ins are free, whereas others are offered for purchase for a small price. To use any of these add-ins you first need to install them.

Inserting an Add-in into a program

1. On the Insert tab, in the Add-ins group, click the My Add-ins drop-down arrow.
2. Click the See All link. In the Office Add-ins dialog box, click Store.
3. Search for the add-in you want, and then follow the directions for installing the add-in.

Access 2016

Access 2016 is a relational database management system to organize, store, and manipulate data. It has four main database objects: tables, queries, forms, and reports. Tables are the fundamental way you store your data. You can create customized forms to input your data and customized reports to summarize data in an easy to read format. Queries allow you to ask questions about your data.

Create a database in Access
1. Open Access 2016 to view the Start screen.
2. Click Blank desktop database. In the Blank desktop database dialog box, name your database, and then click Create.

Note: By default, when you create a new database, Access creates the database with an empty table named Table1, and then opens Table1 in Datasheet view.

Create a table
Tables store data organized in an arrangement of columns and rows. For example, you can create a contacts table to store a list of names, addresses, and phone numbers.
1. On the Create tab, in the Tables group, click Table.
2. On the Fields tab, in the Add & Delete group, click the type of field that you want to add. If you do not see the type that you want, click More Fields.
3. Click the field type that you want.
4. Type the field name.

Use the Query Wizard to create a query
Queries can be used to quickly analyze information in a database. A query allows you to present a question to your database by specifying specific criteria.
1. On the Create tab, in the Queries group, click Query Wizard.
2. If needed, click Simply Query Wizard, and then click OK.
3. In the Tables/Queries list, click to select the table or query on which you want to base the query.
4. Under Available Fields, select the desired fields to add to your query, and then click the > button to add them to the Selected Fields list. Click Next.
5. If needed, click Detail, and then click Next.
6. Enter a title for the query and click Finish.

Use the Form Wizard to create a form
1. On the Create tab, in the Queries group, click Form Wizard.
2. In the Tables/Queries list, click to select the table or query on which you want to base the form.
3. Under Available Fields, select the desired fields to add to your form, and then click the > button to add them to the Selected Fields list. Click Next.
4. Select the layout you want to use for the form, and then click Next.
5. Type a title for the form, and then click Finish.

Note: If you want to fine tune the design of the form, open the form, click the Home tab, click the arrow below View, and then click Design View. Make the changes.

Create a basic report
1. On the Create tab, in the Queries group, click Report Wizard.
2. In the Tables/Queries list, click to select the table or query on which you want to base the report.
3. If you want to group the report on specific fields (for example, you might group a product report on the product type), select the appropriate fields, and click Next.
4. Specify a sort order for the report and click Next.
5. Select the report's layout and orientation and click Next.
6. Type a title for the report and then click Finish.
7. Access saves the report and opens it in Print Preview.

Switch views
1. In the Navigation Pane, right-click on a database object (such as a table) and click Open.
2. On the Home tab, in the Views group, click the View button.
3. Click the command to display the type of view you want to use.

Outlook 2016

Outlook 2016 is a communication program for sending email messages, managing contacts, and maintaining your schedule and task list. Outlook allows you to synchronize your information with mobile devices and Internet services so that you can access your calendar and email anywhere. You can also share your calendar with other people and send meeting requests.

Create and send a new email message
1. If you are viewing your inbox, click the New Email button to create a new email message.
2. In the To text box, type an email address, or click To to select an email address from your address book.
3. Type a subject in the subject text box.
4. In the message area type your message.
5. Click Send.

View the monthly calendar
1. Click Calendar on the Navigation Bar.
2. To view the calendar in month view, click Month in the Arrange group.

Create a new appointment
1. While viewing your calendar in the New group, click New Appointment on the Home tab.
2. Specify the subject, location, start and end times, and an optional description for the appointment.
3. To schedule a recurring appointment, on the Appointment tab, in the Options group, click Recurrence. Use the Appointment recurrence dialog box to specify the appointment time, recurrence pattern, (such as daily, or weekly), and range of recurrence. Click OK to save the changes.
4. On the Appointment Series tab, in the Actions group, click Save & Close.

Schedule a meeting
1. On the Home tab, in the New group, click New Items, and then click New Meeting.
2. Use the To text box to specify the email addresses of the people you want to invite to the meeting.
3. Define a subject, location, and date and time for the meeting.
4. Click Send. Outlook automatically adds the meeting to your calendar and will also do so for all users who accept your meeting invitation.

Add a task to your to-do list
1. On the Home tab, in the New group, click New Items, and then click Task.
2. Type a description of the task in the Subject task box.
3. Optionally, define the task's start date, due date, status, priority, % complete, and whether you want Outlook to remind you about the task.
4. Click Save & Close.

Clutter

In Outlook 2016 for Windows, Clutter helps you filter low-priority email. The email server keeps track of the email you read and the ones you don't. Once you turn it on, Clutter is automatic. As new email comes in, it takes messages you are most likely to ignore and puts them into the Clutter folder.

Note: If you purchased Office 2016 for Windows as a one-time purchase, and you don't have an Office 365 subscription, you won't have access to Clutter.